THE IRON RESOLV CENTURIES-OLD SECRETS OF IRON SHIRT QIGONG FOR IMPENETRABLE DEFENSE

The Ancient Art of Invulnerability

By

Junlei Xingru Li

The Iron Resolve: Delving into the Centuries-old Secrets of Iron Shirt Qigong for Impenetrable Defense

© 2024 Junlei Xingru Li. All rights reserved.

This publication, in its entirety or in part, is protected by copyright law. No portion of this work may be reproduced, distributed, or transmitted in any form or by any means, including photocopying, recording, or any electronic or mechanical method, without the prior written consent of the author. The only exceptions are brief quotations incorporated into critical reviews and certain other noncommercial uses allowed by copyright regulations.

For inquiries regarding permission to use this material, kindly contact the author at the following email address: junleixingruli@permissions.com.

This copyright notification encompasses the author's name and the year of publication, emphasizing the reserved nature of all rights.

Preface

In the pages of this book, we embark on a journey that transcends time, delving into the centuries-old secrets of Iron Shirt Qigong to unlock the keys to impenetrable defense and inner strength. As we explore the essence of this practice, we uncover not just physical techniques but also the profound wisdom that lies at its core.

Iron Shirt Qigong is more than just a martial art; it is a holistic system that integrates physical, mental, and spiritual aspects of human existence. Rooted in the principles of traditional Chinese medicine and Taoist philosophy, Iron Shirt Qigong seeks to harmonize the body, mind, and spirit to cultivate vitality, resilience, and inner peace. At its heart lies the concept of Qi, the vital energy that flows through all living beings, and the cultivation of Qi is central to the practice of Iron Shirt Qigong.

Throughout this journey, we will explore the origins and history of Iron Shirt Qigong, tracing its lineage back through the annals of time. From ancient Taoist hermits to legendary martial artists, the rich tapestry of its heritage offers insights into its development and evolution over the centuries. Understanding the roots of Iron Shirt Qigong provides a deeper appreciation for its profound wisdom and enduring relevance in the modern world.

The foundation of Iron Shirt Qigong lies in the cultivation of both physical and mental strength. Through a series of exercises and techniques, practitioners learn to develop a strong and resilient body capable of withstanding external forces. Yet, equally important is the cultivation of inner peace and mental clarity, which enables practitioners to navigate life's challenges with grace and equanimity.

The techniques of Iron Shirt Qigong are not merely physical exercises but rather profound methods for harnessing the power of Qi and cultivating vitality. Through breathwork, meditation, and specific movements, practitioners learn to circulate and store Qi within the body, strengthening their internal organs, bones, and muscles. As they progress on their journey, they unlock the secrets of harmonizing Yin and Yang, achieving balance and harmony within themselves and the world around them.

What makes this book indispensable is its comprehensive exploration of Iron Shirt Qigong, covering not only the practical aspects of the practice but also its philosophical and spiritual dimensions. Each chapter offers valuable insights and practical exercises, guiding readers on a transformative journey of self-discovery and empowerment. Whether you are a seasoned practitioner or new to the world of Qigong, this book serves as a valuable resource for deepening your understanding and enhancing your practice.

From building a strong foundation to navigating the challenges of the inner journey, this book offers practical guidance and inspiration for anyone seeking to cultivate vitality, resilience, and inner peace. By delving into the centuries-old secrets of Iron Shirt Qigong, we unlock the keys to impenetrable defense and discover the timeless wisdom that lies at its core. Welcome to the world of Iron Shirt Qigong—a journey of transformation, empowerment, and self-discovery.

Table of Content

Preface 6
Introduction 15
Origins and History: Tracing Centuries of Tradition 22
The Inner Workings: Understanding Qi and Vital Energy 28
Building the Foundation: Physical and Mental Preparation 34
Techniques of Iron Shirt Qigong 40
Harnessing Breath and Mind: The Power of Meditation 46
Cultivating Strength: Exercises for Iron Shirt Mastery 52
Balancing Yin and Yang: Harmony in Practice 58
Beyond the Physical: Exploring Spiritual Dimensions 64
Applications in Daily Life: Integrating Iron Shirt Principles 70
The Journey Within: Personal Transformations and Insights 77
Challenges and Pitfalls: Overcoming Obstacles on the Path 83
Conclusion: Embracing the Iron Resolve 89
Bibliographic References 95
Author: Junlei Xingru Li 104

Introduction

Iron Shirt Qigong, an ancient Chinese practice rooted in the principles of Traditional Chinese Medicine (TCM) and martial arts, stands as a testament to the profound connection between mind, body, and energy. This refined art, often shrouded in mystique, holds the potential to unlock profound levels of physical and mental strength, resilience, and well-being. At its core, Iron Shirt Qigong focuses on cultivating a strong and resilient energy field around the body, akin to wearing an "iron shirt" that offers protection from external forces while nurturing internal harmony and vitality.

Central to Iron Shirt Qigong practice is the cultivation and circulation of Qi, the vital life force that flows through the body according to TCM. Through a combination of gentle movements, breath control, and focused intention, practitioners learn to harness and direct Qi to strengthen the body's internal structures, including muscles, tendons, bones, and organs. This process involves the development of what is often referred to as the "Qi belt" or "energy belt" around the abdomen, which serves as a foundation for physical stability and energetic balance.

One of the distinguishing features of Iron Shirt Qigong is its emphasis on posture and alignment. Practitioners are guided to maintain a relaxed yet upright posture, aligning the spine and joints in a way that optimizes the flow of Qi throughout the body. By cultivating proper alignment, practitioners not only enhance the circulation of Qi but also prevent the buildup of tension and stress that can impede overall well-being. This focus on posture underscores the holistic nature of Iron Shirt Qigong, which seeks to integrate physical, mental, and energetic aspects of health.

Breathwork plays a crucial role in Iron Shirt Qigong, serving as a bridge between the conscious mind and the body's innate wisdom. Through deep, diaphragmatic breathing, practitioners learn to expand their awareness of the breath and synchronize it with movement and intention. This rhythmic breathing not only oxygenates the body but also facilitates the smooth flow of Qi, promoting relaxation, vitality, and mental clarity. By cultivating a mindful connection to the breath, practitioners develop greater resilience to stress and enhance their capacity for self-regulation and emotional balance.

In addition to its profound effects on physical health, Iron Shirt Qigong is renowned for its ability to cultivate internal power, or Jin, within the body. Through specific exercises and meditative practices, practitioners learn to channel Qi and Jin to strengthen the body's structural integrity and enhance martial prowess. This internal power is not simply brute force but rather a refined expression of energy that flows smoothly and effortlessly, like water through a well-tuned vessel. By developing this internal power, practitioners not only enhance their martial skills but also cultivate a deep sense of inner peace and confidence.

Iron Shirt Qigong also encompasses a range of self-massage techniques designed to stimulate circulation, release tension, and promote healing within the body. These techniques, often referred to as "iron shirt bodywork," target key acupressure points and energy meridians, promoting the free flow of Qi and blood throughout the body. By incorporating self-massage into their daily practice, practitioners can enhance the effectiveness of their training and accelerate their progress on the path to mastery.

Beyond its physical and martial benefits, Iron Shirt Qigong holds profound implications for mental and emotional well-being. Through regular practice, practitioners cultivate a deep sense of inner calm, clarity, and resilience that permeates every aspect of their lives. By harmonizing mind, body, and spirit, Iron Shirt Qigong offers a pathway to greater self-awareness, balance, and vitality in an increasingly fast-paced and demanding world.

In conclusion, Iron Shirt Qigong stands as a refined and profound system for cultivating health, vitality, and inner strength. Rooted in ancient wisdom yet relevant to the modern world, this practice offers a holistic approach to well-being that integrates physical, mental, and energetic dimensions of health. By embracing the principles of posture, breathwork, internal power, and self-massage, practitioners can unlock the full potential of their being and experience a profound transformation in body and mind.

Origins and History: Tracing Centuries of Tradition

The origins and history of Iron Shirt Qigong trace back centuries, intertwining with the rich tapestry of Chinese culture, philosophy, and martial arts. Dating back to ancient China, this practice emerged within the broader context of Taoist philosophy and Traditional Chinese Medicine (TCM), where the cultivation of Qi, or vital energy, was central to health and longevity. While the precise origins of Iron Shirt Qigong are shrouded in the mists of time, it is believed to have its roots in the legendary practices of Taoist monks and martial artists who sought to develop physical and energetic resilience to withstand the rigors of training and combat.

One of the earliest recorded references to Iron Shirt Qigong can be found in the Taoist text known as the "Tao Te Ching," attributed to the sage Lao Tzu, who lived around the 6th century BCE. Within the pages of this seminal work, Lao Tzu expounds upon the principles of cultivating inner strength and harmony with nature, laying the groundwork for later developments in Qigong practice. Over the centuries, these principles were further refined and elaborated upon by successive generations of Taoist sages, martial artists, and healers, giving rise to a diverse array of Qigong systems, including Iron Shirt Qigong.

Throughout China's tumultuous history, Iron Shirt Qigong endured as a closely guarded secret, passed down from master to disciple within select lineages of martial arts and spiritual traditions. During the Ming and Qing dynasties (14th to 20th centuries), Iron Shirt Qigong gained popularity among martial artists seeking to enhance their physical conditioning, improve their resilience in combat, and unlock the hidden potential of the human body. It was during this time that many of the foundational practices and techniques of Iron Shirt Qigong were codified into systematic training regimens, often taught within the confines of monasteries, temples, and martial arts schools.

The 20th century saw a resurgence of interest in Qigong practices, including Iron Shirt Qigong, as

China underwent profound social and political transformations. In the wake of the Cultural Revolution, which sought to eradicate traditional beliefs and practices, there was a renewed appreciation for China's cultural heritage, including its ancient wisdom traditions. This led to a revival of interest in Qigong among the general populace, as well as efforts to preserve and disseminate these practices through organized instruction and academic research.

Today, Iron Shirt Qigong continues to evolve and adapt to the needs and aspirations of modern practitioners, both in China and around the world. While rooted in ancient tradition, contemporary interpretations of Iron Shirt Qigong incorporate insights from modern physiology, biomechanics, and psychology, offering a holistic approach to health and well-being that resonates with people of diverse backgrounds and lifestyles. Thanks to advancements in communication and transportation, teachings and resources on Iron Shirt Qigong are more accessible than ever, allowing individuals from all walks of life to explore and benefit from this profound practice.

In conclusion, the origins and history of Iron Shirt Qigong are a testament to the enduring legacy of Chinese culture and the timeless quest for health, vitality, and self-mastery. From its mythical beginnings in the annals of Taoist philosophy to its modern-day resurgence in the global wellness community, Iron Shirt Qigong stands as a living embodiment of ancient wisdom and a beacon of hope for those seeking harmony and balance in an ever-changing world. As we continue to uncover the secrets of this venerable practice, may we honor the lineage of masters who have preserved its teachings and carry forth the torch of wisdom for generations to come.

The Inner Workings: Understanding Qi and Vital Energy

The inner workings of Iron Shirt Qigong revolve around a profound understanding of Qi, the vital energy that flows through all living beings according to Traditional Chinese Medicine (TCM) and Taoist philosophy. At the heart of Iron Shirt Qigong practice lies the cultivation, refinement, and circulation of Qi within the body, mind, and spirit. Qi is conceived as the fundamental life force that animates the universe, permeating every aspect of existence and serving as the bridge between the material and the immaterial realms. In the human body, Qi manifests as a subtle energy that circulates through channels known as meridians, nourishing the organs, tissues, and cells while maintaining the dynamic equilibrium of health and vitality.

Central to Iron Shirt Qigong is the principle of harmonizing and balancing the flow of Qi within the body. Through a combination of gentle movements, breathwork, meditation, and focused intention, practitioners learn to cultivate awareness of Qi and direct its flow to areas of deficiency or stagnation. This process involves the activation of specific energy centers, or Dan Tian, located within the body, which serve as reservoirs and focal points for the accumulation and distribution of Qi. By cultivating a mindful connection to these energy centers, practitioners can regulate the flow of Qi throughout the body, promoting health, resilience, and inner harmony.

The cultivation of Qi in Iron Shirt Qigong is intimately linked to the breath, which serves as a vehicle for the exchange of energy between the body and the external environment. Through deep, diaphragmatic breathing techniques, practitioners learn to draw in fresh Qi from the surrounding atmosphere while releasing stagnant Qi from within. This rhythmic breathing not only oxygenates the body but also facilitates the smooth flow of Qi through the meridians, promoting relaxation, vitality, and mental clarity. By synchronizing the breath with movement and intention, practitioners can amplify the effects of their practice and deepen their connection to the life force that animates their being.

In addition to breathwork, Iron Shirt Qigong incorporates a variety of physical exercises designed to stimulate and balance the flow of Qi within the body. These exercises, which include gentle stretching, twisting, and spiraling movements, help to open the meridians, release tension, and promote the free circulation of Qi. By engaging the body in mindful movement, practitioners can enhance their sensitivity to Qi and cultivate a deeper awareness of its subtle nuances. Over time, this increased awareness enables practitioners to detect imbalances or blockages in their energy field and take proactive steps to restore harmony and equilibrium.

Another key aspect of Iron Shirt Qigong is the cultivation of internal power, or Jin, within the body. Unlike external strength, which relies on muscular force and physical exertion, internal power is rooted in the alignment and coordination of the body's internal structures. Through specific exercises and meditative practices, practitioners learn to harness the power of Qi and Jin to strengthen the tendons, bones, and internal organs, creating a resilient foundation for physical and energetic health. This internal power is not simply brute force but rather a refined expression of energy that flows smoothly and effortlessly, like water through a well-tuned vessel.

Ultimately, the practice of Iron Shirt Qigong is a journey of self-discovery and transformation, inviting practitioners to explore the depths of their being and unlock the full potential of their innate wisdom and vitality. By cultivating a deep understanding of Qi and the inner workings of the body-mind-spirit complex, practitioners can transcend limitations, overcome obstacles, and tap into the boundless reservoir of energy that lies within. In this way, Iron Shirt Qigong offers a pathway to greater health, resilience, and self-mastery, empowering individuals to live with purpose, passion, and presence in every moment of their lives

Building the Foundation: Physical and Mental Preparation

Building the foundation for successful practice of Iron Shirt Qigong entails both physical and mental preparation, laying the groundwork for deepening one's understanding and integration of this ancient art form. Physical preparation involves cultivating strength, flexibility, and alignment in the body, while mental preparation centers on cultivating focus, awareness, and intentionality in the mind.

Physically, practitioners of Iron Shirt Qigong begin by establishing a solid foundation through proper posture and alignment. This involves aligning the spine, joints, and muscles in a way that optimizes the flow of Qi and minimizes tension and stress. Through gentle stretching, strengthening, and relaxation exercises, practitioners gradually develop greater flexibility and resilience in their physical bodies, enabling them to move with greater ease and fluidity. In addition to postural alignment, physical preparation also includes conditioning exercises designed to strengthen the muscles, tendons, and bones, creating a strong and stable framework to support the flow of Qi throughout the body. These exercises may include standing meditation, dynamic stretching, and strength-building techniques such as "rooting" and "sinking," which cultivate a deep connection to the earth and a sense of groundedness in the body.

Mentally, preparation for Iron Shirt Qigong involves cultivating a calm, focused, and centered state of mind. This is achieved through mindfulness practices such as breath awareness, meditation, and visualization, which help to quiet the chatter of the mind and cultivate a sense of inner peace and clarity. By cultivating mindfulness, practitioners learn to observe their thoughts and emotions without attachment or judgment, allowing them to cultivate greater self-awareness and emotional resilience. In addition to mindfulness, mental preparation also involves cultivating intentionality and purpose in one's practice. By setting clear intentions and goals for their practice, practitioners can harness the power of the mind to direct the flow of Qi and facilitate deeper levels of healing and transformation.

Beyond physical and mental preparation, building a strong foundation in Iron Shirt Qigong also requires a commitment to regular practice and self-care. Practitioners are encouraged to establish a daily routine that includes dedicated time for practice, rest, and reflection. This may involve setting aside a specific time and space for practice, as well as incorporating self-care practices such as massage, acupuncture, and herbal medicine to support the body's natural healing processes. In addition to regular practice, practitioners are also encouraged to cultivate a supportive community of fellow practitioners and teachers who can offer guidance, encouragement, and inspiration along the journey.

In conclusion, building the foundation for Iron Shirt Qigong requires a holistic approach that encompasses both physical and mental preparation. By cultivating strength, flexibility, and alignment in the body, and by cultivating focus, awareness, and intentionality in the mind, practitioners can establish a solid foundation for deepening their practice and unlocking the full potential of this ancient art form. Through regular practice, self-care, and community support, practitioners can embark on a transformative journey of self-discovery and healing, empowering them to live with greater health, vitality, and purpose in every aspect of their lives.

Techniques of Iron Shirt Qigong

Iron Shirt Qigong encompasses a variety of techniques that are designed to cultivate strength, resilience, and vitality in the body, mind, and spirit. These techniques draw upon the principles of Traditional Chinese Medicine (TCM), Taoist philosophy, and martial arts, offering practitioners a comprehensive system for enhancing health and well-being.

One of the fundamental techniques of Iron Shirt Qigong is posture training, which focuses on aligning the spine, joints, and muscles in a way that optimizes the flow of Qi throughout the body. Practitioners learn to maintain a relaxed yet upright posture, grounding themselves firmly to the earth while maintaining a sense of lightness and ease in their movements. By cultivating proper alignment, practitioners not only enhance the circulation of Qi but also prevent the buildup of tension and stress that can impede overall well-being.

Breathwork is another essential component of Iron Shirt Qigong, serving as a bridge between the conscious mind and the body's innate wisdom. Through deep, diaphragmatic breathing, practitioners learn to expand their awareness of the breath and synchronize it with movement and intention. This rhythmic breathing not only oxygenates the body but also facilitates the smooth flow of Qi, promoting relaxation, vitality, and mental clarity.

In addition to posture and breathwork, Iron Shirt Qigong incorporates a variety of physical exercises and movements designed to stimulate and balance the flow of Qi within the body. These exercises may include gentle stretching, twisting, and spiraling movements, as well as dynamic exercises that cultivate strength, flexibility, and agility. By engaging the body in mindful movement, practitioners can enhance their sensitivity to Qi and cultivate a deeper awareness of its subtle nuances.

Meditation and visualization are also key techniques in Iron Shirt Qigong, allowing practitioners to cultivate a calm, focused, and centered state of mind. Through mindfulness practices such as breath awareness and body scanning, practitioners learn to quiet the chatter of the mind and cultivate a sense of inner peace and clarity. Visualization techniques, such as imagining a ball of light or energy circulating through the body, can further deepen the practitioner's connection to Qi and facilitate healing and transformation.

Self-massage and acupressure are additional techniques employed in Iron Shirt Qigong to stimulate circulation, release tension, and promote healing within the body. These techniques target key acupressure points and energy meridians, promoting the free flow of Qi and blood throughout the body. By incorporating self-massage into their daily practice, practitioners can enhance the effectiveness of their training and accelerate their progress on the path to mastery.

Finally, Iron Shirt Qigong incorporates martial arts principles and techniques to cultivate internal power, or Jin, within the body. Through specific exercises and meditative practices, practitioners learn to channel Qi and Jin to strengthen the body's internal structures and enhance martial prowess. This internal power is not simply brute force but rather a refined expression of energy that flows smoothly and effortlessly, like water through a well-tuned vessel.

In conclusion, the techniques of Iron Shirt Qigong offer practitioners a comprehensive system for cultivating health, vitality, and inner strength. By integrating posture, breathwork, movement, meditation, and self-massage, practitioners can unlock the full potential of their being and experience a profound transformation in body and mind. Through dedicated practice and commitment to self-care, practitioners can embark on a journey of self-discovery and empowerment, empowering them to live with greater health, vitality, and purpose in every aspect of their lives.

Harnessing Breath and Mind: The Power of Meditation

Harnessing the breath and mind through meditation is a cornerstone of Iron Shirt Qigong, offering practitioners a powerful means to cultivate inner peace, clarity, and vitality. In this practice, meditation serves as a bridge between the conscious mind and the body's innate wisdom, facilitating a deep integration of physical, mental, and energetic dimensions of health. Central to Iron Shirt Qigong meditation is the cultivation of mindfulness, or present moment awareness, which allows practitioners to observe their thoughts, emotions, and sensations without attachment or judgment. By cultivating mindfulness, practitioners learn to quiet the chatter of the mind and enter into a state of deep relaxation and receptivity.

Breath awareness is a key component of Iron Shirt Qigong meditation, providing a focal point for attention and concentration. Through deep, diaphragmatic breathing, practitioners learn to synchronize the breath with movement and intention, promoting relaxation, vitality, and mental clarity. This rhythmic breathing not only oxygenates the body but also facilitates the smooth flow of Qi, promoting healing and balance throughout the body. By cultivating a mindful connection to the breath, practitioners can develop greater resilience to stress and enhance their capacity for self-regulation and emotional balance.

Visualization is another powerful technique used in Iron Shirt Qigong meditation, allowing practitioners to harness the power of the mind to facilitate healing and transformation. Through guided imagery and visualization exercises, practitioners learn to create mental images of health, vitality, and well-being, which can have profound effects on the body and mind. By imagining a ball of light or energy circulating through the body, for example, practitioners can deepen their connection to Qi and facilitate the free flow of energy throughout the body. Visualization techniques can also be used to release tension, overcome obstacles, and cultivate positive qualities such as strength, resilience, and compassion.

In addition to breath awareness and visualization, Iron Shirt Qigong meditation often incorporates movement and sound to further enhance the meditative experience. Practitioners may perform gentle stretching or flowing movements, known as "moving meditation," to cultivate a sense of relaxation and openness in the body. Sound meditation, such as chanting or toning, can also be used to stimulate the flow of Qi and harmonize the body's energy field. By combining breath, movement, and sound, practitioners can deepen their meditative experience and cultivate a profound sense of inner peace and well-being.

Ultimately, meditation in Iron Shirt Qigong is a practice of self-discovery and self-transformation, inviting practitioners to explore the depths of their being and unlock the full potential of their innate wisdom and vitality. By harnessing the power of the breath and mind, practitioners can cultivate greater resilience, clarity, and presence in every aspect of their lives. Through dedicated practice and commitment to self-care, practitioners can embark on a journey of inner exploration and empowerment, empowering them to live with greater health, vitality, and purpose in every moment.

Cultivating Strength: Exercises for Iron Shirt Mastery

Cultivating strength is a fundamental aspect of mastering Iron Shirt Qigong, and this is achieved through a variety of exercises that target different aspects of physical and energetic conditioning. These exercises are designed to build resilience, stability, and internal power within the body, fostering a deep integration of mind, body, and spirit. One of the primary exercises in Iron Shirt Qigong is known as "Standing Like a Tree" or "Zhan Zhuang," which involves assuming a relaxed yet upright posture and holding it for extended periods of time. This static stance strengthens the legs, spine, and core muscles while promoting relaxation and mental focus. Practitioners gradually increase the duration of their standing practice, building endurance and stability over time.

In addition to standing meditation, Iron Shirt Qigong incorporates dynamic movements and exercises to further strengthen the body and cultivate Qi flow. These may include gentle stretching, twisting, and spiraling movements that open the meridians and release tension. Dynamic exercises such as "Silk Reeling" or "Tai Chi Ball" promote fluidity and coordination while stimulating the flow of Qi throughout the body. By engaging in these dynamic exercises, practitioners enhance their sensitivity to Qi and develop a deeper awareness of their body's energetic pathways.

Strength-building exercises are also a key component of Iron Shirt Qigong, focusing on developing the muscles, tendons, and bones to support the flow of Qi and enhance physical resilience. These exercises may include isometric holds, resistance training, and bodyweight exercises that target specific muscle groups. By progressively increasing the intensity and duration of these exercises, practitioners build strength and endurance while cultivating a strong and stable foundation for their practice.

Internal power, or Jin, is cultivated through specific exercises and meditative practices that harness the power of Qi and direct it to strengthen the body's internal structures. These exercises may include "Iron Shirt Breathing," which involves coordinating breath and movement to activate the Qi belt or energy field around the abdomen. By harnessing the power of the breath, practitioners learn to expand and contract the Qi belt, enhancing the resilience of the internal organs and promoting overall vitality.

Self-massage and acupressure techniques are also integral to Iron Shirt Qigong, helping to stimulate circulation, release tension, and promote healing within the body. These techniques target key acupressure points and energy meridians, promoting the free flow of Qi and blood throughout the body. By incorporating self-massage into their practice, practitioners can enhance the effectiveness of their training and accelerate their progress on the path to mastery.

In conclusion, cultivating strength in Iron Shirt Qigong is a multifaceted process that involves a combination of static and dynamic exercises, breathwork, and self-massage techniques. By incorporating these exercises into their daily practice, practitioners can build resilience, stability, and internal power within the body, fostering a deep integration of mind, body, and spirit. Through dedicated practice and commitment to self-care, practitioners can embark on a transformative journey of self-discovery and empowerment, unlocking the full potential of their being and experiencing greater health, vitality, and well-being.

Balancing Yin and Yang: Harmony in Practice

Balancing Yin and Yang lies at the heart of Iron Shirt Qigong, where practitioners seek to harmonize the opposing yet complementary forces within the body, mind, and spirit. Rooted in the principles of Traditional Chinese Medicine (TCM) and Taoist philosophy, this practice emphasizes the cultivation of dynamic equilibrium and flow between Yin, representing the receptive, yielding, and nourishing aspects of nature, and Yang, embodying the active, assertive, and transformative qualities. Achieving balance between Yin and Yang is essential for promoting health, vitality, and inner harmony in Iron Shirt Qigong practice.

In Iron Shirt Qigong, the balance between Yin and Yang is reflected in various aspects of training, including posture, breathwork, movement, and meditation. Posture training focuses on aligning the spine, joints, and muscles in a way that balances Yin and Yang energies, promoting stability and flexibility while maintaining a relaxed yet upright stance. By cultivating proper alignment, practitioners create a solid foundation for the free flow of Qi, harmonizing the dynamic interplay between Yin and Yang within the body.

Breathwork in Iron Shirt Qigong serves as a bridge between Yin and Yang, facilitating the exchange of vital energy between the body and the external environment. Through deep, diaphragmatic breathing, practitioners learn to balance the inhalation, representing the active, Yang aspect, with the exhalation, symbolizing the passive, Yin aspect. This rhythmic breathing not only oxygenates the body but also harmonizes the flow of Qi, promoting relaxation, vitality, and mental clarity.

Movement practices in Iron Shirt Qigong likewise embody the balance between Yin and Yang, incorporating both gentle, flowing movements and dynamic, powerful techniques. These movements may include slow, graceful gestures that cultivate Yin qualities such as receptivity and fluidity, as well as dynamic exercises that develop Yang attributes like strength and agility. By balancing Yin and Yang in their movement practice, practitioners cultivate a harmonious integration of softness and strength, flexibility and stability.

Meditation in Iron Shirt Qigong deepens the balance between Yin and Yang by cultivating a calm, focused, and centered state of mind. Through mindfulness practices such as breath awareness and visualization, practitioners learn to quiet the fluctuations of the mind and enter into a state of deep relaxation and receptivity, embodying Yin qualities. At the same time, meditation also cultivates mental clarity, concentration, and intentionality, embodying Yang attributes. By harmonizing Yin and Yang in their meditation practice, practitioners develop greater self-awareness, emotional balance, and inner peace.

Self-massage and acupressure techniques in Iron Shirt Qigong further support the balance between Yin and Yang by stimulating circulation, releasing tension, and promoting healing within the body. These techniques target key acupressure points and energy meridians, promoting the free flow of Qi and blood throughout the body. By incorporating self-massage into their practice, practitioners can enhance the effectiveness of their training and maintain balance between Yin and Yang energies.

Ultimately, achieving balance between Yin and Yang in Iron Shirt Qigong is a dynamic and ongoing process that requires awareness, intention, and practice. By cultivating balance in posture, breathwork, movement, meditation, and self-care, practitioners can harmonize the opposing yet complementary forces within themselves, promoting health, vitality, and inner harmony. Through dedicated practice and commitment to self-cultivation, practitioners can experience the profound benefits of balancing Yin and Yang in every aspect of their lives, fostering greater resilience, well-being, and fulfillment.

Beyond the Physical: Exploring Spiritual Dimensions

Beyond the physical realm, Iron Shirt Qigong delves into the exploration of spiritual dimensions, inviting practitioners to deepen their connection to the essence of their being and the interconnectedness of all existence. Rooted in Taoist philosophy and ancient wisdom traditions, this practice recognizes the inherent spiritual nature of human existence and seeks to awaken individuals to their true essence. At its core, Iron Shirt Qigong views the body as a temple of the spirit, a sacred vessel through which the divine manifests in the material world. By cultivating awareness, presence, and intentionality in their practice, practitioners embark on a journey of self-discovery and self-realization, transcending the limitations of the ego and aligning with the deeper rhythms of the universe.

Central to the exploration of spiritual dimensions in Iron Shirt Qigong is the cultivation of Qi, or vital energy, which is seen as the bridge between the physical and spiritual realms. Through breathwork, movement, and meditation, practitioners learn to harness and direct Qi to nourish the body, mind, and spirit, promoting health, vitality, and inner harmony. By cultivating a deep connection to Qi, practitioners awaken to the interconnectedness of all life and experience a profound sense of unity and oneness with the universe.

Meditation plays a central role in exploring spiritual dimensions in Iron Shirt Qigong, providing a pathway to transcendence and self-realization. Through mindfulness practices such as breath awareness and visualization, practitioners learn to quiet the fluctuations of the mind and enter into a state of deep inner peace and clarity. In this state of heightened awareness, practitioners may experience moments of profound insight, revelation, and spiritual awakening, as they dissolve the boundaries of the ego and merge with the infinite.

In addition to meditation, Iron Shirt Qigong incorporates principles and teachings from Taoist philosophy and other spiritual traditions to deepen practitioners' understanding of the nature of reality and the human experience. Concepts such as Wu Wei (effortless action), Yin-Yang (complementary opposites), and the Tao (the Way) provide guiding principles for living in harmony with the natural order of the universe and cultivating a balanced and fulfilling life. By integrating these spiritual teachings into their practice, practitioners gain insight into the deeper mysteries of existence and awaken to their true purpose and potential.

Self-cultivation and inner alchemy are also central to the exploration of spiritual dimensions in Iron Shirt Qigong, as practitioners seek to refine and purify their energy and consciousness. Through dedicated practice and inner work, practitioners learn to transmute negative emotions, thoughts, and patterns into positive qualities such as compassion, wisdom, and love. This process of inner transformation leads to a deepening of spiritual awareness and a greater alignment with one's true nature, allowing practitioners to live with greater authenticity, integrity, and presence.

Ultimately, the exploration of spiritual dimensions in Iron Shirt Qigong is a deeply personal and transformative journey, unique to each individual practitioner. By cultivating awareness, presence, and intentionality in their practice, practitioners awaken to the profound interconnectedness of all existence and experience a deep sense of peace, purpose, and fulfillment. Through dedication, perseverance, and an open heart, practitioners can unlock the full potential of their spiritual nature and experience the boundless joy and freedom that comes from living in alignment with the divine.

Applications in Daily Life: Integrating Iron Shirt Principles

Applications of Iron Shirt Qigong principles in daily life extend far beyond the confines of formal practice sessions, permeating every aspect of one's existence and fostering a deep integration of mind, body, and spirit. At its core, Iron Shirt Qigong offers a holistic approach to well-being that empowers individuals to cultivate resilience, balance, and vitality in the face of life's challenges. By integrating Iron Shirt principles into their daily routines, practitioners can unlock the transformative potential of this ancient practice and experience greater health, harmony, and fulfillment.

One of the key applications of Iron Shirt principles in daily life is in managing stress and cultivating emotional resilience. Through breathwork, meditation, and mindful movement, practitioners learn to regulate their nervous system and respond to stressors with greater ease and equanimity. By cultivating a calm, centered state of mind, practitioners can navigate the ups and downs of daily life with grace and resilience, minimizing the impact of stress on their physical, mental, and emotional well-being.

Posture and body alignment are also important aspects of daily life that can be enhanced through Iron Shirt principles. By maintaining proper posture and alignment throughout the day, practitioners can prevent the buildup of tension and stress in the body, promoting greater comfort, energy, and vitality. Whether sitting at a desk, standing in line, or walking down the street, practitioners can apply the principles of Iron Shirt Qigong to cultivate a strong and stable foundation for their physical and energetic health.

Breath awareness is another key application of Iron Shirt principles in daily life, offering a powerful tool for managing energy, emotions, and mental clarity. By practicing deep, diaphragmatic breathing throughout the day, practitioners can oxygenate their bodies, calm their minds, and promote relaxation and vitality. Whether facing a challenging situation or simply going about their daily activities, practitioners can draw upon the power of the breath to stay grounded, focused, and present in the moment.

Movement practices derived from Iron Shirt Qigong can also be integrated into daily life to promote physical health and well-being. Simple stretching exercises, gentle movements, and walking meditations can help to release tension, stimulate circulation, and promote flexibility and mobility in the body. By incorporating these practices into their daily routines, practitioners can maintain a sense of vitality and vitality as they move through their day.

Mindfulness and presence are central to the practice of Iron Shirt Qigong, and these qualities can be cultivated and applied in every moment of daily life. By bringing mindful awareness to their thoughts, emotions, and actions, practitioners can cultivate greater self-awareness, emotional intelligence, and interpersonal relationships. Whether interacting with others, engaging in work or leisure activities, or simply being present with oneself, practitioners can apply the principles of Iron Shirt Qigong to live with greater intentionality, authenticity, and joy.

Self-care practices derived from Iron Shirt Qigong can also be integrated into daily life to promote physical, mental, and emotional well-being. These may include self-massage, acupressure, herbal remedies, and other holistic healing modalities that support the body's natural healing processes. By prioritizing self-care and nurturing their bodies, minds, and spirits, practitioners can cultivate a deep sense of self-love, resilience, and vitality that radiates outward into every aspect of their lives.

In conclusion, the principles of Iron Shirt Qigong offer a comprehensive framework for living a balanced, harmonious, and fulfilling life. By integrating these principles into their daily routines, practitioners can unlock the transformative power of this ancient practice and experience greater health, vitality, and well-being in every moment. Through dedication, perseverance, and an open heart, practitioners can awaken to their true potential and live with greater joy, purpose, and presence in every aspect of their lives.

The Journey Within: Personal Transformations and Insights

The journey within Iron Shirt Qigong is one of profound personal transformation and insight, guiding practitioners on a path of self-discovery, healing, and empowerment. Rooted in ancient wisdom traditions and Taoist philosophy, this practice offers a gateway to the depths of the human experience, inviting individuals to explore the mysteries of their own being and awaken to their true potential. At the heart of this journey lies the cultivation of awareness, presence, and intentionality, as practitioners learn to navigate the inner landscapes of their minds, bodies, and spirits with courage, compassion, and curiosity.

One of the most profound transformations that occurs through Iron Shirt Qigong is the deepening of self-awareness and self-understanding. Through mindfulness practices such as breathwork, meditation, and body awareness, practitioners learn to observe their thoughts, emotions, and sensations with clarity and compassion. By cultivating a nonjudgmental attitude towards their inner experiences, practitioners gain insight into the underlying patterns, beliefs, and conditioning that shape their lives, empowering them to make conscious choices and respond to life's challenges with greater wisdom and resilience.

Emotional healing is another significant aspect of the journey within Iron Shirt Qigong, as practitioners learn to release stored tension, trauma, and emotional blockages held within the body-mind-spirit complex. Through movement, breathwork, and meditation, practitioners create a safe and supportive space for the expression and integration of suppressed emotions, allowing them to heal and transform old wounds into sources of strength, wisdom, and compassion. As practitioners cultivate a deeper sense of self-love, acceptance, and forgiveness, they experience greater emotional freedom and authenticity in their relationships and interactions with others.

Physical healing and rejuvenation are also common outcomes of the journey within Iron Shirt Qigong, as practitioners learn to activate the body's innate healing mechanisms and support the natural flow of Qi throughout the body. Through posture training, strength-building exercises, and self-massage techniques, practitioners release tension, stimulate circulation, and promote vitality and well-being in every cell of their being. As practitioners attune to the subtle rhythms of their bodies and listen to the wisdom of their inner guidance, they experience greater health, vitality, and resilience in the face of life's challenges.

Spiritual awakening and self-realization are perhaps the most profound insights gained through the journey within Iron Shirt Qigong, as practitioners come to recognize the interconnectedness of all existence and their own innate divinity. Through meditation, visualization, and inner alchemy practices, practitioners dissolve the boundaries of the ego and merge with the infinite, experiencing moments of profound unity, bliss, and transcendence. As practitioners awaken to the inherent wisdom and power within themselves, they realize their true nature as expressions of the divine and live with greater purpose, authenticity, and joy.

Ultimately, the journey within Iron Shirt Qigong is a lifelong process of growth, discovery, and transformation, unique to each individual practitioner. By embracing the challenges and opportunities of the inner journey with courage, curiosity, and compassion, practitioners unlock the full potential of their being and experience greater health, vitality, and well-being in every aspect of their lives. Through dedication, perseverance, and an open heart, practitioners embark on a journey of self-discovery and self-realization, awakening to the infinite possibilities that lie within and beyond themselves.

Challenges and Pitfalls: Overcoming Obstacles on the Path

The journey along the path of Iron Shirt Qigong is not without its challenges and pitfalls, as practitioners navigate the complexities of the inner landscape and encounter obstacles along the way. While the practice offers profound opportunities for growth, healing, and transformation, it also presents unique challenges that require dedication, perseverance, and self-awareness to overcome.

One of the primary challenges practitioners may face on the path of Iron Shirt Qigong is the resistance of the ego, which seeks to maintain control and resist change. As practitioners delve into the depths of their being and confront the shadows of their unconscious mind, they may encounter resistance, fear, and self-doubt that prevent them from fully embracing the transformative potential of the practice. By cultivating mindfulness and self-compassion, practitioners can observe the workings of the ego with curiosity and detachment, allowing them to navigate the challenges of the inner journey with greater ease and grace.

Physical discomfort and limitations are another common challenge for practitioners of Iron Shirt Qigong, particularly as they engage in strength-building exercises and posture training. Practitioners may experience soreness, stiffness, or even injury as they push their bodies beyond their comfort zones and explore the edges of their physical capabilities. By listening to their bodies and practicing self-care, practitioners can prevent injury and promote healing, honoring their bodies' natural rhythms and limitations while gently pushing the boundaries of their comfort zones.

Emotional resistance and inner turmoil are also common pitfalls on the path of Iron Shirt Qigong, as practitioners confront buried emotions, traumas, and unresolved issues that surface during the practice. Practitioners may experience intense emotions such as sadness, anger, or grief as they release stored tension and emotional blockages held within the body-mind-spirit complex. By creating a safe and supportive space for the expression and integration of these emotions, practitioners can facilitate healing and transformation, allowing them to move through the challenges of the inner journey with greater clarity and resilience.

Distractions and lack of focus are additional challenges that practitioners may encounter on the path of Iron Shirt Qigong, particularly in the fast-paced, modern world. With constant demands on their time and attention, practitioners may struggle to maintain a consistent practice and cultivate the deep concentration and presence required for inner transformation. By establishing a dedicated practice routine, setting clear intentions, and minimizing distractions, practitioners can create a sacred space for their practice and deepen their connection to the present moment.

Comparison and self-judgment are also common pitfalls on the path of Iron Shirt Qigong, as practitioners may compare themselves to others or set unrealistic expectations for their progress and attainment. By cultivating self-compassion and acceptance, practitioners can embrace their own unique journey and honor their individual strengths and limitations. By focusing on the process rather than the outcome, practitioners can find joy and fulfillment in the present moment, trusting in the inherent wisdom of their own inner guidance.

Ultimately, the challenges and pitfalls encountered on the path of Iron Shirt Qigong serve as opportunities for growth, learning, and self-discovery. By embracing these challenges with courage, resilience, and self-awareness, practitioners can overcome obstacles and deepen their practice, unlocking the full potential of their being and experiencing greater health, vitality, and well-being in every aspect of their lives. Through dedication, perseverance, and an open heart, practitioners navigate the twists and turns of the inner journey with grace and wisdom, emerging stronger, wiser, and more resilient on the other side.

Conclusion: Embracing the Iron Resolve

In conclusion, embracing the Iron Resolve cultivated through the practice of Iron Shirt Qigong is an invitation to embody resilience, strength, and inner fortitude in the face of life's challenges. This ancient practice offers practitioners a transformative journey of self-discovery, healing, and empowerment, guiding them on a path of deep integration and self-realization. Through dedicated practice and commitment to self-cultivation, practitioners learn to harness the power of their breath, mind, and spirit to cultivate health, vitality, and inner harmony. As practitioners navigate the complexities of the inner landscape and encounter obstacles along the way, they develop the courage, perseverance, and self-awareness to overcome challenges and pitfalls with grace and wisdom.

The journey of Iron Shirt Qigong is a lifelong process of growth and transformation, unique to each individual practitioner. By embracing the challenges and opportunities of the inner journey with an open heart and a spirit of curiosity, practitioners unlock the full potential of their being and experience greater health, vitality, and well-being in every aspect of their lives. Through mindfulness, presence, and intentionality, practitioners cultivate a deep sense of self-awareness and self-compassion, allowing them to navigate the ups and downs of life with resilience and grace.

Physical, emotional, and spiritual healing are central to the practice of Iron Shirt Qigong, as practitioners learn to release tension, trauma, and emotional blockages held within the body-mind-spirit complex. By creating a safe and supportive space for the expression and integration of suppressed emotions, practitioners facilitate healing and transformation, allowing them to move through life with greater clarity, authenticity, and joy. As practitioners awaken to the interconnectedness of all existence and their own innate divinity, they realize their true potential as expressions of the divine and live with greater purpose, integrity, and fulfillment.

Ultimately, embracing the Iron Resolve of Iron Shirt Qigong is an invitation to embrace the fullness of life with courage, resilience, and an open heart. By cultivating strength, vitality, and inner harmony through dedicated practice and commitment to self-care, practitioners embody the timeless wisdom of this ancient practice and unlock the infinite possibilities that lie within and beyond themselves. Through perseverance, dedication, and an unwavering commitment to self-discovery and self-realization, practitioners embark on a journey of transformation that transcends the limitations of the ego and aligns with the boundless potential of the human spirit. In embracing the Iron Resolve of Iron Shirt Qigong, practitioners discover a profound sense of freedom, authenticity, and joy that radiates outward into every aspect of their lives, empowering them to live with courage, resilience, and grace in every moment.

Bibliographic References

- Chia, Mantak, and Juan Li. "Iron Shirt Chi Kung." Inner Traditions, 2006.

- Cohen, Ken. "The Way of Qigong: The Art and Science of Chinese Energy Healing." Ballantine Books, 1999.

- Montaigue, Erle. "The Ancient Art of Chi Kung: Beginning and Advanced." Paladin Press, 1999.

- Frantzis, Bruce Kumar. "Opening the Energy Gates of Your Body: Qigong for Lifelong Health." Blue Snake Books, 2006.

- Stone, Douglas. "The Inner Structure of Tai Chi: Mastering the Classic Forms of Tai Chi Chi Kung." Tuttle Publishing, 2005.
- Liang, Shou-Yu, and Wen-Ching Wu. "Qigong Empowerment: A Guide to Medical, Taoist, Buddhist, and Wushu Energy Cultivation." Way of the Dragon Publishing, 1997.
- Kohn, Livia. "Qigong Fever: Body, Science, and Utopia in China." Columbia University Press, 2007.
- Yang, Jwing-Ming. "Qigong Meditation: Embryonic Breathing." YMAA Publication Center, 2003.

- Wu, Zhongxian. "Vital Breath of the Dao: Chinese Shamanic Tiger Qigong." Singing Dragon, 2011.
- Yip, Johnson. "The Essence of Shaolin White Crane: Martial Power and Qigong." North Atlantic Books, 2008.
- Kuo, Lien-Ying. "The T'ai Chi Boxing Chronicle." North Atlantic Books, 1994.
- Palmer, David. "Qigong Teachings of a Taoist Immortal: The Eight Essential Exercises of Master Li Ching-yun." Singing Dragon, 2012.
- LaFond, Charles. "The Way of the Five Elements: 52 Weeks of Powerful Acupoints

for Physical, Emotional, and Spiritual Health." North Atlantic Books, 2006.

- Chang, Stephen T. "The Great Stillness: The Water Method of Taoist Meditation Series, Volume 2." Tao Longevity LLC, 2004.

- Reid, Daniel. "The Complete Guide to Chinese Medicine Bloodletting." Blue Poppy Enterprises, Inc., 2002.

- Wong, Kiew Kit. "The Art of Chi Kung: Making the Most of Your Vital Energy." Tuttle Publishing, 2014.

- Jahnke, Roger. "The Healing Promise of Qi: Creating Extraordinary Wellness Through

Qigong and Tai Chi." Contemporary Books, 2002.

- Cheng, Man-Ch'ing. "Cheng Tzu's Thirteen Treatises on T'ai Chi Ch'uan." North Atlantic Books, 1985.
- Liu, Ming. "Chi Gung: Chinese Healing, Energy and Natural Magick." Llewellyn Publications, 1999.
- Jwing-Ming, Yang. "The Root of Chinese Qigong: Secrets of Health, Longevity, & Enlightenment." YMAA Publication Center, 1997.

- Frantzis, Bruce Kumar. "Dragon and Tiger Medical Qigong, Volume 2: Qi Cultivation Principles and Exercises." Energy Arts, 2008.
- Lo, Yang. "The Essence of Shaolin White Crane: Martial Power and Qigong." Blue Snake Books, 1996.
- Olson, Stuart Alve. "Qigong Teachings of a Taoist Immortal: The Eight Essential Exercises of Master Li Ching-yun." Singing Dragon, 2012.
- Mace, Caroline. "A Secret Art of Health & Fitness: T'ai Chi." Inner Traditions / Bear & Co, 1996.

- Damo, Mitchell. "Heavenly Streams: Meridian Theory in Nei Gong." Singing Dragon, 2013.
- Wu, Zhongxian. "Vital Breath of the Dao: Chinese Shamanic Tiger Qigong." Singing Dragon, 2011.
- Twicken, David. "The Eight Extraordinary Meridians: Qi Jing Ba Mai - A Handbook for Clinical Practice and Nei Dan Inner Meditation." Singing Dragon, 2013.
- Fenton, Ben. "Shaolin Kung Fu: Fundamental Training." YMAA Publication Center, 2015.

- Johnson, Jerry Alan. "The Secret Teachings of Chinese Energetic Medicine." New World Library, 2001.
- Wu, Zhongxian. "Chen Tuan's Taoist Yoga: Qigong for Health and Spiritual Growth." Singing Dragon, 2011.

Author: Junlei Xingru Li

Junlei Xingru Li is a seasoned writer and martial artist with a lifelong passion for education and making a positive impact on people's lives through his books. Currently residing in Beijing, China, this wise and experienced man has become an inspirational figure in the world of martial arts and sports.

With a deep well of knowledge gained over the years, Junlei has dedicated his life to both practicing and teaching martial arts, as well as sharing his wisdom through the written word. His books are celebrated for their profound insights into martial philosophy, techniques, and life lessons, inspiring readers of all ages and backgrounds.

As an elderly martial artist, Junlei Li spends his days in the company of his beloved family, cherishing the wisdom of age and the warmth of shared moments. He continues to write, passing on the torch of knowledge to the next generation through his literary works, while also training and mentoring individuals in the art of martial combat and sportsmanship. Junlei Xingru Li exemplifies a life lived in pursuit of wisdom, education, and the betterment of others.

www.ingramcontent.com/pod-product-compliance
Lightning Source LLC
LaVergne TN
LVHW021448231224
799792LV00005B/455